THE LIVABLE AND THE UNLIVABLE

The Livable and the Unlivable

A CONVERSATION INITIATED
BY ARTO CHARPENTIER
AND LAURE BARILLAS

TRANSLATED BY ZAKIYA HANAFI

Judith Butler
Frédéric Worms

FORDHAM UNIVERSITY PRESS   NEW YORK 2023

This book was originally published in French as Judith Butler and Frédéric Worms, *Le vivable et l'invivable*, published by Presses universitaires de France (PUF), 2021. The Afterword is original to the English edition.

Fordham University Press has no responsibility for the persistence or accuracy of URLs for external or third-party Internet websites referred to in this publication and does not guarantee that any content on such websites is, or will remain, accurate or appropriate.

Fordham University Press also publishes its books in a variety of electronic formats. Some content that appears in print may not be available in electronic books.

Visit us online at www.fordhampress.com.

Library of Congress Cataloging-in-Publication Data available online at https://catalog.loc.gov.

Printed in the United States of America

25 24 23   5 4 3 2 1   -

First edition

Contents

PREFACE   vii

Introduction
By Arto Charpentier and Laure Barillas   1

The Livable and the Unlivable   11

Afterword   43

NOTES   77

Preface

"This is not a life." In March 2018, close to two thousand migrants were living in makeshift camps in northern Paris, scattered along the banks of the canal, on the sides of the beltway, and under highway bridges. Sleeping in tents, or simply under blankets, lacking adequate food distribution and access to water, they endured conditions of severe deprivation.

"This is not a life," they might well have said to deplore their situation. This is not a life, and yet it is one, because, although unlivable, these lives are no less lived: it is an unlivable and yet *living* life. As Judith Butler writes, "this very doubling indicates that this life is not yet extinguished, that it persists in formulating a demand and a claim, precisely in the name of its *living* character":[1] the conditions necessary for its continued presence and activity must be secured, here and now. Frédéric Worms reminds us of this need for a "vital hospitality" that is irreducible to survival. A proper response to these situations requires "the establishment of a *minimum right (droit) among humans* that first preserves the absolute minimum in all spheres of relations between humans and life, but also the law (*droit*)."[2]

When we speak about unlivable lives, then, we refer to a "conceptual contradiction that is nevertheless lived," suggests Butler, and turn this contradiction into an instrument of social and political critique. To describe these lives as unlivable is to assert that they should not be lived, not like this; put differently, it means to decry the scandal of the conditions to which they are subjected and to express the urgent need for their redress.

This is the backdrop for the exchange between Judith Butler and Frédéric Worms that took place on April 11, 2018, at the École Normale Supérieure (ENS) in Paris.[3] It continues their collaborative reflection first embarked on at ENS in 2015[4] and resumed the following year, this time at the University of California at Berkeley.[5] In comparing their philosophical approaches, both thinkers evoke the possibility of transforming this vital emergency into a positive claim that creates a new norm for political action: that of securing everyone the conditions of a livable life.[6]

THE LIVABLE AND THE UNLIVABLE

Introduction

Laure Barillas and Arto Charpentier

What resources can a philosophy of the living provide to a critical sociopolitical philosophy today? This is the question that underlies the exchange between Judith Butler and Frédéric Worms held at the École Normale Supérieure (Paris) in April 2018.[1] Their discussion around a shared theme—the livable and the unlivable—sheds light on how their work has developed from opposing directions. Starting from a philosophical reflection on the living inspired by his reading of Bergson and Canguilhem, Frédéric Worms laid the groundwork for a "critical vitalism,"[2] in which care is pivotal to his political, even cosmopolitical, thought. Judith Butler, inspired by Hegel and Foucault, began rather from a critique of social and political norms and their subjugating effects,[3] which they elaborated in an exploration of the precariousness of human lives. This work has led today to what they call a social ontology of the living body.[4] These reversed paths across a common problem—life and power—from the living to the social for Worms and from the social to the vital for Butler, is what we were particularly interested in probing.

Their dialogue on the unlivable brings this convergence to the fore: for both, the act of social and political criticism is rooted in bodies and their imminent needs. The reason they both move away from an existential conception of lives in their recent works[5] is certainly because "existence" entails a more distant, less pressing relationship to bodies than "life" or "the living." Thus, in their work political reflection ties into a philosophy of life. Although they do not go so far as Simone Weil in proposing a list of the essential needs of the body and soul, they do nonetheless formulate a normative aspiration that can serve as a guide for politics: the aspiration to ensure each and every living human the conditions of a livable life (but without prescribing in advance what this life must be).

As soon as they make the distinction between the livable and the unlivable the normative compass of their sociopolitical criticism, however, they are necessarily faced with a series of questions: How are we to distinguish between the livable and the unlivable? What criteria should be used to make this distinction? And how are we to justify the choice of the criteria in question? This is an important issue at stake in a philosophical gesture such as theirs: the moment they base their sociopolitical criticism on a division between the livable and the unlivable, they have no choice but to specify the basis on which this distinction is made.

We will therefore try to situate this dialogue in the evolution of their thought, by examining how their unique sociopolitical philosophies have led them to engage with questions related to life; and how, in return, a reflection on living humans provides their sociopolitical philosophy with the resources to find its bearings in today's world.

From the Vital to the Social: Frédéric Worms's Critical Vitalism between Polarity and Care

What is Frédéric Worms's "critical vitalism" and how does it entail a *critical* sociopolitical philosophy?

Heir to the vitalism of Bergson and Canguilhem, Worms's philosophy draws equally on the psychoanalysis of Freud and Winnicott and on the ethics of care: all sources for thinking about relations between living humans. His main concern is to understand the vital significance of moral and political relations between human beings. The method he uses is critique, to which Worms gives three meanings:[6] first, he understands it as *refusal*, since he defines life in the tradition of Bichat, as that which resists death; second, as *discernment*, since we know life only through differences between living creatures; and, finally, as *reflexivity*, since he seeks an ethical and political criterion for understanding what is vital.

Critical vitalism is articulated around two central concepts: *polarity* and *care*. Polarity, like critique, refers directly to the works of Canguilhem. In *The Normal and the Pathological*, Canguilhem defines life as a *critical* activity, in the sense that it is an immanent position of values.[7] For Canguilhem, a living organism is fundamentally a normative being: by its dynamic reactivity, it establishes a polarity between conditions that support the continuation of its life, which are assigned a positive vital value, and those that are harmful to its activity, which receive a negative value. According to Canguilhem, there is a normativity (the possibility to establish norms) inherent in all living beings. Worms's "critical vitalism" inherits from Canguilhem's legacy and extends it: philosophical reflection, he suggests, must also take this vital normativity as its compass—including when it confronts sociopolitical issues.

Critical vitalism thus conceives of life as polarized, cut across by tensions that cannot be reduced to any single substance or principle. For Worms, the *vital* refers less to the Bergsonian vital impulse than to a vital minimum: a sociopolitical guarantee of the "vital minima" that make lives livable. Worms lays out three main polarities that structure the act of criticism: between life and death, between attachment and violation, and between care and power. These polarities are not "external, between life *and something else*; [they] are internal, even consubstantial, to life *as such*":[8] indeed, all living beings are mortal, no attachment relationships are immune from the risk of violence and violation, and all care practices are permeated by power dynamics. So, while critical vitalists, faithful to vital normativity, take a decisive stance in favor of life, attachment, and care, they nevertheless recognize that these tensions are constitutive and impossible to circumvent. The concept of polarity, like that of critique, evokes this ambivalence that is intrinsic to all vital phenomena and to which care responds.

Critical vitalism uses the concept of care specifically to make sense of social relations between the living. Care is not limited to the ethics of care or to the theory of holding developed by Donald Winnicott. Theories of care, especially Carol Gilligan's, reiterate the need to make concern for others and a willingness to help and support them central rather than peripheral to a theory of justice. For his part, Winnicott calls for all aspects of care to be taken into account, including the psychological and political dimensions that enable the subject's emergence through the acts of "carrying," "holding," and "presenting to the world."[9]

To Canguilhem's polarity of the vital and the mortal Worms adds that of creation and destruction, inspired by Winnicott. The critical character of Worms's vitalism leads him to view relationships as destructive or dominating as well as creative and supportive. Worms defines care as "a relationship between people that is subjective and even creates subjectivity (without which we would not be individuals). It is a moral but also social relationship and, therefore, already political: a relationship with the world and even a concern for the world that is equally natural and cultural, ecological, and political."[10] The sociopolitical thought he has developed on care goes beyond the framework of medicine or the parent-child relationship and invites a new ethico-political reflection on justice. Care is rescue and support, but it is also *power*, which must be recognized, and *work*, which must be critiqued.

Understandably, then, when life is deprived of care, in all its forms (support, work, solidarity, concern), it is made unlivable. The possibility of care, insofar as it also implies the political and social institutions that underpin it, is the first criterion of a life's livability. A life without care is a body whose survival is endangered, a damaged subjectivity, the principles of justice undermined, and an obstructed concern for the world. Worms describes the deep solidarity that links care to politics as "care for care, support for support, recognition of relations of recognition, power over relations of power."[11] This brings the link he makes between care and democracy to the fore: in his vision, care extends to the safeguarding of democratic principles and even takes on an ecological and cosmopolitical scope in a contemporary concern for justice and the world.

Precarious Lives and Social Criticism in Judith Butler: From the Social to the Vital and Back

Butler's approach to issues about the living comes from the opposite direction: it was their sociopolitical examination on the impact of power and social norms on living bodies that led them to reflect on the question of life.

Starting from their earliest writings on gender,[12] Butler has sought to show how certain social norms exclude individuals and entire groups from the possibility of social recognition, thereby depriving them of the social means necessary to lead a livable existence. Indeed, according to Butler, those who are excluded from dominant social norms are subject not only to symbolic and moral disqualification but also to various forms of discrimination that expose them to increased forms of social and economic insecurity, and to heightened risks of violence and injury.

Implicit in their early work on the social regulation of gender is a reflection on the precarity of lives, which they later developed and expanded.[13] Through the concept of precarity, Butler seeks to describe the social processes through which certain populations are actively supported, defended, and protected, while others are abandoned or exposed deliberately to heightened risks of suffering, illness, violence, and death. These risks are not simply a matter of natural fatality; they are the result of social and political dynamics that reveal the different values any given society places on human lives. For Butler, all lives are precarious, but some are more precarious than others, and it is impossible to disentangle *precariousness*, understood as a shared existential condition, from *precarity*, i.e., the social and political processes that put specific populations differently at risk, endangering their life expectancy.[14]

Against the exclusion in principle of all that has to do with the living body and the conditions of its preservation outside the public sphere (and their relegation to a private, supposedly apolitical sphere), Butler invites us on the contrary to recognize "bodily dependency and need, hunger and the need for shelter, the vulnerability to injury and destruction, forms of social trust that let us live and thrive, and the passions linked to our very persistence, as clearly political issues."[15]

This claim is illustrated by the recent mobilizations against precarity, which they analyze in *Notes Toward a Performative Theory of Assembly*. From Occupy Wall Street to Black Lives Matter to the mobilizations against gender violence, these movements differ in their methods and goals. But what they have in common is that they formulate their demands "in the name of the living body, one entitled to life and persistence, even flourishing"; they thus place the question of "livable life" at the forefront of politics.[16]

Politics cannot escape the pressing question of the social conditions of life, and from *Precarious Life* on, Butler has unhesitatingly mined our condition as living beings for the philosophical insights it provides. In *Frames of War*, they thus set forth a "social ontology" of the body, which aims at describing the relational conditions of our embodied existence.[17] For Butler, a living human being (and perhaps a living being *in general*) is always *ex-static*, in the sense that it is necessarily "outside" or "beyond" itself: it cannot survive or flourish without being sustained by a set of heterogeneous relations that provide the conditions for its persistence and activity.[18] Talking about *social* ontology is thus the way for Butler to situate the living body in relation to material, infrastructural, intersubjective, and, more generally, social and environmental conditions, without which this body can hope neither to survive nor to flourish.

Butler's philosophical reflection on the living thus supports and underpins their sociopolitical critique. In *The Force of Nonviolence*, Butler affirms vulnerability and interdependence as constitutive qualities of the living creatures that we are, and they elucidate the ethico-political obligations that stem from them. Ultimately, this is the critical requirement that Butler believes must serve as the norm for political action:

> to secure the conditions for livable lives, and to do so on egalitarian grounds. This would imply positive obligations to provide those basic supports that seek to minimize precariousness in egalitarian ways: food, shelter, work, medical care, education, rights of mobility and expression, protection against injury oppression.[19]

The Democracy of the Living

Despite their opposing departure points, Worms and Butler are now united in basing their sociopolitical reflection on a social philosophy of the living (*social* in the sense that this philosophy never separates the living from the historically specific social relations and institutional arrangements that condition its persistence and activity). They both believe that "our interdependence on one another" requires "a public organization of all;[20] that is, a set of social, economic, and political conditions and institutions that ensures everyone the conditions of a livable life. Both thinkers maintain that this requirement defines democracy, understood not only as a political regime but more broadly as a form of life.

In *Assembly*, Butler argues that there can be no true democracy without the conditions for radical equality among human lives, and that, conversely, the primary responsibility of a democratic government is to guarantee and strengthen the conditions for that equality.[21]

Worms speaks of a "vital democracy." He observes that "democracy is like life":[22] it is not only a form of political government but, above all, a moral and social aspiration that must permeate all human relations. Democracy is vital insofar as it is required by care; indeed, through care we "will sustain not just one person, but the world, not just a few, but each and every one, all people, the whole world."[23] Democracy, just like care, is the only political framework that can guarantee subjects the possibility of being themselves, that supports their relational dimension, which acts as a bulwark against the violations that threaten them. In other words, what democracy and care have in common is the twofold requirement of equality and justice.

Democracy is therefore the regime in which lives are given equal dignity and equal support to subsist and flourish. But, Worms suggests, just as care can turn into abuse, democracy can make lives unlivable. These are what he calls the "chronic diseases of democracy": cynicism, racism, and ultraliberalism, which deprive some lives of the conditions necessary to live their lives as their own.[24] The inherent polarity of democracy is thus this permanent risk of regression and violation against which we must fight relentlessly.

Finally, on the basis of his critical vitalism, Worms proposes to revisit the values of democracy: fraternity (understood as the recognition of this vital interdependence, which obligates us) must lead to a struggle for equality between lives, which itself has no other end than the liberty (or autonomy) of each person.[25]

Butler agrees with this need for freedom as a condition for a livable life. For them, democracy, as a form of shared life, demands an effort to secure everyone the conditions of a livable life, without prescribing in advance what that life must be. Hence their preference for the term safeguarding, rather than preservation: "safeguarding is not quite the same as preserving," they write in *The Force of Nonviolence*, "though the former presupposes the latter: preserving seeks to secure the life that already is; safeguarding secures and reproduces the conditions of becoming, of living, of futurity, where the content of that life, that living, can be neither prescribed nor predicted, and where self-determination emerges as a potential" to be safeguarded.[26] The democratic aspiration thus includes the concern of ensuring all living beings the effective possibility to decide by themselves, without illegitimate interference, the concrete modalities of their existence and its flourishing. According to Butler, this is a defining requirement of life: without this possibility of creation and experimentation, they write, "a life is merely existing; but it is not living."[27]

Judith Butler and Frédéric Worms both anchor their social and political reflection in a thought of what the living, in its precariousness and fragility, requires of us. They believe that recognition of the relationality and interdependence that constitute human lives must lead to formulating a demand for radical equality between living humans, which translates into a democratic effort to ensure each person the conditions for a livable life, without pronouncing on the concrete form that this life will take.

By making a truly *livable* life the normative horizon of their practical philosophies, they point to a struggle against precarity that aims at expanding the conditions of solidarity between the living, in a world that is equally livable for all. Finally, this democratic practice, along with its urgency and difficulty, appears to be the task of "the living whose open and fragile lives are oriented towards politics, but whose fragile and open politics remains oriented by life."[28]

The Livable and the Unlivable

Arto Charpentier: Our preliminary question would be "What is the unlivable?" Would you agree in defining it as that which we cannot live in or live through? At the same time, we must also investigate what the unlivable is. Is it merely survival, or does a life need to be more than survival to be truly livable? If that's the case, then where does the threshold lie between the livable and the unlivable? And what, in your opinion, are the sociopolitical implications of this distinction?

Frédéric Worms: It's such a pleasure for me to have this opportunity to discuss an issue that runs throughout Judith's work but without yet being made fully explicit, perhaps. I believe it is a shared problem that we tackle from different perspectives, a problem that is itself in some sense *vital*.

Judith Butler: It's a kind of a strange declension of "living." Simply put, the livable is a condition of life that can be lived, whereas the unlivable is a condition of life that cannot be lived.

FW: Some might say "viable," but we may have the chance to talk about this difference between viability (purely biological, in essence) and livability (a notion that cannot be reduced to a strictly biological level, although it points toward what is *vital* for us).

JB: Yes. In English, at least, debates about the fetus as viable make it hard, but not impossible, to use that word.

FW: What we are discussing, then, is a criterion that allows us to distinguish between the livable and the unlivable, and the importance of being able to define such a criterion, since everyone has claims about the "unlivability" of a particular experience or life, and we must be able to adjudicate these claims. One often hears people say: "It's unlivable," but who is justified in saying it?

The question is important for another reason, which relates to the place these concepts have in Judith's philosophical and political work as a whole, beginning with *Gender Trouble*. In that book, the claim is made on behalf of certain lives that are made "unlivable" because of some normative or political situation. Starting there, we must ask ourselves: can we—and how can we—define a criterion of sorts to distinguish between the livable and the unlivable? I would like to start by examining three separate hypotheses. I'll reject the first one completely; I'll retain an essential point from the second, which strikes me as central to Judith's approach; but I'll complete it with a third hypothesis that, in my opinion, is indispensable for defining the livable and the unlivable.

I'll be brief as far as the first hypothesis is concerned, which I characterize by its method. At first glance, it would appear to be the easiest approach for distinguishing between the livable and the unlivable, because it argues that we should rely on the description of an experience, of particular experiences, to look at what happens to us or to certain people, and then say: "This is livable; that, on the other hand, is unlivable." This is what I call, very simply, the phenomenological approach. We act as if someone could describe various experiences and say: "This is livable" (or even "This is what the livable looks like") and, by contrast, "That is unlivable" (or even "That is what the unlivable looks like"). This would be the first methodology, an apparently spontaneous one, for arriving at a precise distinction between the livable and the unlivable. I think, as you may have guessed, that this is a mistake based on an impossibility in principle, and I imagine that Judith would agree on this point. Why is it an impossibility in principle? For one simple reason, which gives us, by contrast, our first criterion for the unlivable. This is a first approach by antithesis, but it may very well give us an essential distinction, and by that I mean that the opposite is true: if something is unlivable, then someone cannot live it and, even less, describe it.

In reality, there is no way you can ask someone to describe the unlivable. If they can describe it, then it is not (the present tense is important) unlivable. This provides us with a fundamental clue leading to the criterion of the unlivable, which must be defined by the impossibility *for someone*, for a *subject*, to live it. At a minimum, the unlivable is precisely the fact that the life cannot, or can no longer, be the life of someone who can describe it; it cannot be a subjective life, the life of someone who lives their life. This is the first criterion, which is still a negative one, but won't this term necessarily be defined in the negative? The unlivable is not something that can be lived by someone and described by them; rather, it precludes their emerging from life and living their life. This is our first criterion, whose importance is signaled by its enormous impact.

From this we can immediately infer the second hypothesis, which consists once again of a definition of the unlivable and the livable. We will say that the conditions of "livability" are the conditions of subjectivity. The condition of livability is the condition for a life to be the life *of someone*. Livability begins with the possibility that a subjective "self" emerges, that someone can "live" what is thus "a" life or "their" life. These conditions could be psychological, social, or political, for example, and we thus enter into the realm of what Judith calls "recognition" (following in the wake of others, beginning with Hegel). This is crucial, but is it enough? Let's come back to this question later.

We therefore start from the fact that for life to be livable, it must be *someone's* life. Intersubjectivity—one person's recognition of another as the subject of "their" own life—may and almost certainly will enter into the conditions of this livability. But the essential still lies beneath this: in the pure and simple emergence of a "self" that has to live "its" life. This includes acts such as representing one's life to oneself, thinking about it and narrating it, and of course, having it recognized. But all this depends on something else, which is very precise and radical: the conditions of livability are the empirical conditions of subjectivity in the most general sense, although it then involves further levels. These conditions of livability are not just "biological," they are psychological, social, and political. Judith Butler's work is crucial for understanding how the life of "someone" can, or cannot, emerge from all sorts of conditions. For of course, by their absence, denial, or destruction, the conditions of livability also define those of its opposite: unlivability is also a very concrete possibility.

It must therefore be stated forcefully from the outset: unlivability is not a theoretical abstraction; the unlivable is possible. There are lives that are impossible to live, and the question we are now going to consider is whether unlivability is comparable to death. Ultimately, what do these two ways of making life impossible—unlivability and death— have in common? This is a key question, in my view, and I will come back to it, but for now, let us take our bearings. The unlivable and the livable have conditions, subjective or intersubjective, social, political, moral, and certainly linguistic, among others. The impossibility of describing the unlivable pointed to this aspect: the unlivable is also unspeakable, and if we want to talk about it, at the very least there will be a detour involved, a price to pay, a contradiction that will arise in language itself; conversely, livability undoubtedly has to do with the capacity to express it, to speak, and thus involves language.

This leads us to what I believe is the risk of this second stage, this second position, if we fail to immediately supplement it. This is the question I've also been fortunate enough to discuss with Judith for some time now. It can be formulated very simply: If we understand the livable and the unlivable to be that which can or cannot be lived by a subject, what then remains of life? Where is life in itself? This is the question that remains to be answered.

We must take it at its word; that is to say, understand if it is simply a matter of words. The criterion we have now is the emergence of a self, a subject, a someone. But this is the criterion of what we call the "livable" as opposed to the unlivable. Is the fact that the word "unlivable" is etymologically related to "life" philosophically relevant or not? That is the question. Judith posed this very question when they asked: What is the difference, and is there one, between that which is "unlivable" or "intolerable" and that which is livable and tolerable? Here we hit on the most critical point: Is there anything specific to the unlivable as such, and what is its relationship to life and to that which is vital? Can we really omit life from the criterion for distinguishing between the livable and the unlivable?

The fact that the criterion can involve the psychological, the social, and the political does not mean that it is not ultimately vital. Nor does it mean that unlivability should not be conceived of starting from a material or biological model, in the strict sense of someone's life and its opposite, death. The unlivable must be a sort of interruption of what we call our bodily life or our vital conditions. Let's state upfront that it must involve a destruction of the self that is like death, and if there's an analogy, it's not that it's "less" than death but, rather, worse than death, precisely because the life goes on but what makes it a life or allows someone to live it is dead—a death that manifests by the destruction, disappearance, interruption of life, modeled on the interruption of the movements (in our brain) that defines death. It must be something similar to and worse than death, since "life" continues without "someone" to live it. The reason we call it unlivable is because it's like the interruption of life, the interruption of our vital conditions. It must not be a distinction of degree but of kind, not quantitative but qualitative and critical, and, truth be told, it is at the core of what I call "critical vitalism."

This is why I claim to be a follower of Canguilhem or Bergson, both of whom start from a qualitative difference. Canguilhem rejected the idea that the difference between "the normal and the pathological" can be understood as a simple matter of degree. Either it is absolute, qualitative, and subjective, or it does not exist at all. As I see it, the same

applies to the difference between the livable and the unlivable. Later on, there can be degrees. Bergson showed this
clearly: once we have gone from A to B, we can reconstitute
a path—the degrees or stages between the two. But before
measuring degrees, one must begin by establishing the qualitative difference, since we cannot do otherwise. The same
goes for the distinction between the normal and the pathological, which, according to Canguilhem, is a subjective
polarity that is irreducible to a quantitative difference: even
though, afterwards, it can be translated into averages or
thresholds, as in biological analyses.

We therefore need a qualitative criterion for the unlivable; but ultimately, by the same token, we have it: given to
us by the opposition between life and death, or rather the
opposition of life "to" death, but extended to the life "of
someone." And this takes place in an "intersubjective" and
literally vital interaction, since it allows or does not allow,
influences or destroys, the emergence of a "self" in a particular living being in relation to others. This may be the case
for all the living: maybe every living being is at the same
time a "someone" that lives a life but may also not live it, that
may find themselves stripped of the conditions for living it
while remaining "alive," that may "die" in the very concrete
sense that "they" can no longer live it. It is not "death," but
it is "their" death. What allows us to see it? Perhaps the fact
that they no longer see us. That which lives in them is therefore dead. We have used the same criterion of life here as we
do for all other vital functions, in a doubly "critical" way: a
purely qualitative, polarized criterion; something that is
either there or it is not; but it cannot be reduced to a single
level or single function.

We've arrived at the core of critical vitalism.

We need a criterion that distinguishes between the livable and the unlivable that is both vital and critical. This

brings us back to critical vitalism, which takes the opposition between life and death literally (in the sense that Deleuze gives to this term: beyond the opposition between the proper and the figurative, beyond any metaphor or image), but which (as Derrida would have put it) sees "more than one" form in it.

There is more than one form of death in the life of any living being, especially living humans, and that is why we talk about the unlivable. There are also multiple forms of the unlivable, which result in the death of the subject whose life it was. And just as we can die, in the classical sense of the word, from hunger or cold, so our life can be made unlivable (and therefore mortal) by a lack of recognition, by depression or melancholy, by more than one cause, or in more than one way. And just as human life consists in taking care of the living against death, it also consists in taking care of the livable against the unlivable, in arranging for the conditions of a livable life in all senses, in all the vital dimensions of living humans.

There are three consequences to this. First of all, it is clear that unlivability must continue to be modeled on death. Death is the unlivable in both the objective sense and the subjective sense. Epicurus expressed this in terms of logic: when we are dead, we are no longer alive. Being alive and being dead oppose each other, they contradict each other, giving rise in philosophy to many seemingly self-evident statements or truisms (what we call "verités de La Palice" in French) that, curiously, we seem to come back to again and again. As was said of La Palice: "He died on Friday, the last day of his life / If he had died on Saturday, he would have lived longer." Sartre said of himself that "Death will never get me alive," and Ricoeur wrote: "I'll live up to death." It's as if this logical contradiction could and should be assigned a different vital value each time.

But the unlivable is not simply death, in general. It is a specific form of death. Just as I cannot "live" death, similarly and conversely, when I can no longer live an experience, it is like death, because life continues but "I" cannot live it: the experience of the unlivable has destroyed the subject of life, what Simone Weil calls the "soul" in her book on misfortune.[1] Ultimately, it is not the soul, since the soul cannot be destroyed; but it is indeed the living subject, which can be destroyed. In the same way, when Judith asked me whether I "took seriously the phrase of *social death* as describing slavery in Orlando Patterson's work on slavery as social death?" I said that I did, of course. "Social death" is, indeed, the most accurate way to express it. Durkheim defined suicide as a "social fact," which is what a certain form of social death (anomie, in his view) leads to. In the case of slavery, the enslaver would seek to go as far as destroying the slave's subjectivity. Indeed, this destruction of the self is a real possibility. In cases of extreme violations, subjectivity can actually be destroyed. I understand this destruction literally, as a form of death.

This leads us to what Derrida, following Adorno and Lyotard, calls "worse than death." There are experiences similar to death that are not only unlivable but worse than death. The unlivable is worse than death, because even if this life goes on, this person cannot live it as their life but only as death within life. Hence the tragic end-of-life choices and political issues: dilemmas in which one has to choose between death and something worse than death.

Those who live these experiences cannot describe them, and this is precisely why others are obligated to do so. If we talk about them, it is not because we live the unlivable but because we have the obligation to describe the unlivable lives of those who are living them and, by definition, cannot talk about them.

Finally, if there is something worse than death then there is something more than life and better than the livable. The livable is not an ultimate norm. We want to live lives that are not just livable but also happy and joyful. We want to live fully: meaning, a life in which all dimensions of life (the biological, the intersubjective, the creative and symbolic . . .) are unified. Each of these dimensions can be destroyed, which is the possibility that the concept of the unlivable aims to describe. There is something more than the livable, then: more than the ability to move or not to die but, rather, to be the creative and social subject of one's life.

Consequently, the opposite of destruction and "worse than death" is something "more than simply living," and that is necessarily creativity, in Donald Winnicott's sense, since, for him, "the place where we live" is the place of ordinary creation in our lives—that fundamental, intermediate zone where our subjectivity can transform the world, even if minimally. But one last point deserves emphasis: the place of critique in life as such, in our living being. The philosophy of critical vitalism includes a negative polarity in life, and, therefore, since there are degrees in the living, it also includes in the living the negative task of criticizing whatever threatens "livability."

Unlivability can be individual, relational, or common; for example, when the state of the world is a common unlivability that threatens us all. What is an unlivable world? It is a world that is unlivable for all of us, due to environmental or political reasons; unlivability is certainly not restricted to individual lives.

So, the issue we need to discuss with Judith, if we agree on my criticism of the phenomenological approach and on the political and subjective conditions of real life, is about integrating the vital and the critical. Let me finish by coming back to the vital, since life is present everywhere in Judith

Butler's work, in the titles of several of their books, such as *Precarious Life*. But should we take it literally? Is the opposition of the livable and the unlivable a primary concept? That's my question.

JB: OK, thank you very much, Frédéric, and thank you, Laure and Arto, for your introduction, and thank you all for coming here today. Frédéric suggests that I have many answers but I'm not sure I do have many answers. I am nevertheless happy to pursue his questions and hopefully that will be useful for us and for the further conversation. First of all, Frédéric is absolutely right that there is a persistent question of how best to distinguish between the livable and the unlivable, what criterion does one use in order to make that distinction, and how would one then in turn justify the use of that criterion. In general, I don't have a fully formulated answer to that question, although I do think that some answers are embedded in the analyses that I try to provide. So maybe one task for me is to think about how to extract the implicit criteria that are operating in the analyses and make that conceptually clear. When we ask about the distinction between the livable and the unlivable, one question, the easier question, might be: "How do you know it? How do you know the difference between the livable and the unlivable?" But I want to reformulate this problem as the following cluster of questions: How is the distinction made? What kind of judgement is used in order to make that distinction when it is made? Who makes it, in relation to whom? What is the scene or the situation historically, politically, in which that judgment is made again and again; that is, both made and contested? Because it seems to me we can certainly cite all kinds of geopolitical zones where a legal determination is made that the refugee situation is absolutely unlivable and others would say, "Oh no, they're being processed and everything is, you know, just going a little slowly: it's too bad, we are working on a shelter, should be available soon, etc."

So, you know, sometimes there is a contest about who is making the designation of livability for what purpose and in what institutional setting. So that's one question I have, do we need to situate the judgement, who makes it, through what language, and to what effect? I just suggested legal determinations could be one way in which that judgement is made and contested. That would of course not be quite the same as philosophical distinctions of the sort you are looking for between the livable and the unlivable. But maybe we need to examine the different practices of judgement that exist, which are making or failing to make that distinction, and try to analyze them in terms of how they operate and what they are effectively doing or not doing. This means that I do not start with the conceptual distinction but ask whether it is embedded in the practices of judgment, and whether we can discern its operation there. I also wonder: even if we were to come up with a single criterion—let's say I didn't sidestep your question and tried to answer it straight forwardly, let's say I came up with a single criterion . . . And I'm going to try to do that for you because I think it will make you happy (laughs).

FW: Good idea!

JB: 'Cause I'm a good guest. (laughs)

But look, seriously, even if we came up with such a criterion, would it be ours to make here and now; in other words, would it be a conceptual contribution that intellectuals make? In what language would it be formulated? What difference would it make which language it is in, and would it be translatable among all languages? In other words, would it retain its singularity, or would it turn out to have different variations? By languages I don't just mean natural languages like English and French but also linguistic practices that involve understanding who is speaking and to whom, and about whom, in what situation, for what purpose, and what happens with the language after it is entered into the world, which is sometimes—very often—not fully anticipated.

So that's one cluster of problems I have with your question. I understand why you want to set aside quickly the phenomenological approach and not ask the question: "Is there a subject who can describe the unlivable and are we then dependent on that subject's description in order to know what the unlivable is?" And you want to set that aside, as I understand it, in order to ask a different question, which is what are the conditions of subjectivity that make possible the distinction between the livable and the unlivable? So, your expectation as I understand it from this exposition and from other texts I read from you, is that if we go into these conditions of subjectivity, which are for you, I believe, empirical conditions, we will find the criterion there. It would have to be a feature characteristic of the subjective conditions of a life.

But here is where I have a least two points. I do think that descriptions of the unlivable, and here I am thinking about testimony, the kind of testimony we get from, say, Charlotte Delbo, about Auschwitz, is a testimony to the unlivable. I am not sure we can conclude that it was not unlivable for her precisely because she was able to give a testimony. In other words, I don't think it's a contradiction in terms to go through the unlivable, to write about it, and writing includes the lapse of language, the silence, the white page, the non-narrative structures, which we often see in testimony that is seeking to convey traumatic material. The narrative "I" can index a shattered or destroyed subjectivity even as it relays what is seen. The distinction between author and narrator does not require, for instance, the repair of the author. So I would not doubt that Charlotte Delbo went through the unlivable and just because she was able to use language in some ways—and it took her some time to return to whatever language she did have—that does not mean that what she went through was not unlivable. Look, she was alive, she was writing. That doesn't refute the postulation. And in fact, it could well be that the kind of writing we have from her, the kinds of descriptions we receive of or from the unlivable, are a window onto the structure of subjectivity that you are interested in. She reports that she can recall only from a certain perspective at a distance from reliving. Is she not broken? Are there not conditions under which people break? And if, broken, they still live on, that does not mean that they are living a livable life. No, not at all. So, if this is true that the broken person can narrate the traumatic past, and the narrative itself does not repair the break, if the broken person narrates from the break itself, then we have designated a kind of living on under conditions in which the unlivable also lives on with you and at the same time. That kind of living on is not the same as the survival of the self. One is living on and yet the unlivable still lives with you or accompanies you without any expectation of its ending. It ends only when life ends. Whatever of your life is left is lived with the unlivable as its companion or its constitutive wreckage, perhaps as an unbearable companion from which separation is impossible. So I don't think that's necessarily a contradiction—living on, in, and with the unlivable.

Perhaps the case of Delbo can turn our attention to the question of the relationship between what we called the unlivable and language. For instance, under certain conditions we call something an unlivable experience. At that moment, we understand ourselves as right to call it that way, whether it is something we have undergone or some other person, or group of persons. There are debates about this. Some would argue that if someone goes through an unlivable experience then it is something that is not quite available to consciousness or to language. According to that version of trauma theory, the unlivable is the rupture in experience. If it is narrated in some way, then this rupture or this break in experience, a break in the continuity of experience, must also be brought to language in some way, and without being covered over or sutured by the narrative. Hence, the question "What is the relationship between the unlivable and language?" is specified as one that seeks to know the status of narrative in relation to the problem of representing trauma, when trauma is defined at least in part (or in full) as a rupture in continuity. Do there need to be (have there already been?) non-narrative forms, or forms of descriptions that can in some ways evoke or resonate with the traumatic as such? Or does there have to be a distance, a dissociated distance, from the phenomenon in order to give it a linguistic or narrative version?

That said, I would want to say first that unlivability is not the same as death, although it maintains a vital relationship to death, vital in the sense of indispensable, and that the phenomenological description, which is invariably a description in language or through a medium of some kind—it could be through sound, image, or texture, or any number of forms of representation—can contain in itself an understanding of the coexistence and the simultaneity of living on with the unlivable, without resolving the unlivable into the livable. So, if you want to argue that conceptually the livable and the unlivable are opposed, then we have to take account of their simultaneity within the phenomenological field. I belabor this point because of the increasingly popular use of the term *resilience* to describe what happens to migrants, for instance, who are abandoned at sea, or what happens to people who are kept in indefinite detention, or people who have been bombarded in a military conflict. They are not always bouncing back, regardless of their occasional collaborative moments of creative resistance (and those surely exist).

Resilience is of course a term that certain kinds of humanitarian and human rights organizations use to talk about the possibilities of—in English we say, "bouncing back," finding resources to overcome difficulty, even resuming a former life even though one has been through this very terrible situation. This term, resilience, belongs to a neoliberal vocabulary that looks away from human destruction and destitution; it tends to presume in advance that people are never definitively broken, that there is no such thing as a break or rupture in a life, that the breaking of a person or the rupture of a life never affects the capacity, presumably inherent, to rise up again, to affirm and resume life. Whatever version of the life force the discourse of resilience relies upon operates as a kind of metaphysical guarantee, a quick recourse to optimism, and perhaps a kind of denial and lie. We see how the term enters public policy imperatives that are given to non-governmental organizations and how it propagandizes a conception of the person as flexible, bendable, endlessly resurrectable, even though, or precisely when, certain kinds of breakages and losses are actually irreversible and stay with people throughout their lives, destroying their sense of life. And even if they live on, living on with the unlivable is not the same as resilience. No, not at all. In effect, I worry that the term "resilience" operates to deny reality and repress trauma, and that it all too quickly sees and attributes the potential of reparation when it is clearly no longer possible.

OK, that was perhaps a polemical aside.

It does, however, bring me back to the subject; that is, the supposition that we are talking about a subject who undergoes an unlivable experience and who can name that experience in the course of undergoing it or after having undergone it. It might be one sign that the experience was unlivable that the subject is deprived of a language to name it as such or struggles with a language in which to name it. But the converse is not true: sometimes there can be language for the unlivable, which does not mean that the experience has become livable. Language is not the measure, the criterion. The situation changes, however, when the unlivable experience is shared, even though it may not be right to say that it registers in the same way for each person who goes through it. People are pushed onto boats together, they are abandoned at sea together, they are bombed together, and the survivors have all lost family members, or neighbors, or friends and lovers. If an unlivable experience is shared (differently shared), does it become any more livable by virtue of having been shared? We talked earlier today about refugee activism, migrants who are gathered on the border without proper shelter, without healthcare or nutrition, who understand themselves as undergoing an unlivable experience together even as they also produce communication networks and modes of interdependency in order to provide the support they are emphatically *not* getting from public or state or international institutions and agencies.

When the conditions can be assessed or understood together, what difference does that make, or start to make, among those who are undergoing or have been undergoing an unlivable experience? And one thing I would say is that the condition of the subject, the condition of subjectivity, to use Frédéric's language, in situations such as these is also a condition of intersubjectivity—and that latter word is an important word. When we refer phenomenologically to intersubjectivity, that is not the same as a collective subject in which all differences are erased; rather, it refers to a differentiated network or a differentiated group that lives through and comes to assess and understand a common situation together. "Where did you get your cell phone?" or "I heard there was food over here." Or "We are organizing and going to the fence together in order to make a political claim." So, when there is a kind of shared unlivability, if we can speak that way, it seems to me that something about human interdependency, the dependency on food, shelter, mobility, legal services, and so something about livability as a function of human sociality is brought to the fore.

It's those aspects of life that I think make life more livable; that is, if it is organized according to norms that seek to safeguard and further livability. The condition which Frédéric calls subjective is for me a condition that I would call intersubjective, an understanding that the self does not emerge or persist without a supportive infrastructure for human interdependency. When we are faced with shared conditions of unlivability, I would ask what is the failure in economic and social infrastructures, international institutions and obligations (including maritime law), or of communities or nations? Where are those failures, and how did they come about, such that people have been left or abandoned or exposed to violence? How would we seek to restore or repair, or build for the first time, the intersubjective institutional conditions which would include conditions for the possibility of cohabitation such that life could become increasingly livable for populations deprived of that possibility?

The reason the subject has to be referred to intersubjectively is that my life is not livable without your life being livable, without a number of lives being livable, because we are commonly dependent on each other and social structures for common life. The subject that I am is dependent on care not only in infancy but throughout life, and "care" is meant here less as a maternal disposition than a social and institutional provision for a livable life. When the structures that we depend upon fail, we also fail and fall. And though our devastations are registered individually as events in our lives, including our psychic lives, those losses and failures are in fact to some degree shared, to some degree social, economic, political. So, if we want to interrogate the conditions of the livable and the conditions of the unlivable, we have to turn to the institutional support, to infrastructures that nourish the living.

What's more, these conditions of interdependency without which livable life is impossible also imply principles of equality, not the equality of independent persons as they are measured with one another, not precisely an equality among individuals. Rather, what I have in mind is an equality that describes the mutually dependent relations of people in social and economic life. Equality, then, as a feature and result of interdependency.

If I am right, then the intersubjective conditions of livable life imply a kind of obligation toward the life of the other, one that is owed me as well. The obligation follows from the social relations that define the individual and decenter its claim. My life is bound up with your life without any contract that stipulates that to be the case. It is bound up as well with those lives I do not know, whose language I do not speak, who live at a great distance from where I live. There's no such thing as my life without those other lives. To say that there is, is precisely to misunderstand what a self is. Once one understands that defining and binding interconnection, one that is limited neither by community nor nation, then one can more easily approach both a political and economic understanding of equality, an equality that would provide the criterion for the fight against the unequal distribution of wealth, the intensification of precarity in certain regions of the world. One could approach as well the ethical obligation that I argue is one of nonviolence, which is not just to protect the life of the other, but to affirm and to support the institutional conditions that support interdependent lives as part of a community without borders, one that would not be communitarian, that would not be nationalist, that would not reduce to religious affiliation or parochial and exclusionary forms of secular self-understanding. With that framework in mind, we could perhaps start to move toward the criterion that would distinguish between the livable and the unlivable, but that would take us in another direction. I want to be able with you to understand conditions of livability, but I am less sure how to answer the question of life as such. I don't know about life as such. What do I know? I don't know.

FW: You tell us.

JB: No, that is yours to tell (laughs).

FW: Thank you for these openings. I'd like to respond briefly. Of course, beyond the opposition between the livable and the unlivable, there are uses or practices of this opposition, ways of working with it and expressing it. For example, the narrative of the survivor, of someone who has gone through the experience of the unlivable and must confront both the livable—since they're in the process of writing—but also the unlivable—since they seek to give an account of the past unlivability that they've lived through. But I would argue that a narrative is not a description. Telling a story is not the same as describing, especially when it's about an unlivable experience or trauma, but rather a different way of grasping it. And this is done through the limits of the narrative and the unnarratable, which is actually an aspect of the unlivable. The narrative of the unlivable has its own special characteristics: it, too, is broken from inside.

You can't tell a story about a trauma the way you tell an anecdote: it would distort the truth of what happened. So, there are some specific characteristics in the narratives of Charlotte Delbo, Primo Levi, and Varlam Chalamov that must be examined. Practices of this opposition are also in the social practices of the refugees we were talking about, and in the vital response of human beings caught in this contradiction, even in extreme situations in which they've built some livability within unlivable experiences. For my part, I have also criticized the notion of resilience if it is applied aggressively and ignores contexts in which it becomes an abstract concept of resurrection.

In any case, these practices do not nullify this opposition. On the contrary, they confirm it, because the narratives of refugees and survivors—the state of "living on" (or *sur-vivre*) that Derrida wrote about—which is both living and dying at the same time, do not nullify it. The inseparability of the two notions does not nullify their opposition and tension.

My question is thus the following: If there are practices that do not nullify the contradiction, does it remain a vital ontological and philosophical criterion? Is it still essential to found this opposition on life as such, on the unlivable as such?

True, the opposition of the livable and the unlivable is not a "foundation" but rather an appeal: it calls for our criticism, our action, our expression through art, literature, and cinema. But the fact remains that this contradiction needs to be set down as such, and we need philosophy to develop it as such. Because there is no "foundation" beyond it—for example, in some hypothetical essence of "life." This opposition serves as a compass for all others, and its critical use is what should orient us in understanding practices that are vital for us, as in the case of the concrete lives of refugees, because they are caught in this contradiction. Our culture would like us to forget that there really are lives in the grip of the unlivable. It would like to have either the victims (the dead) or the living released from this opposition. But it's there and it concerns us all, and we need it to get our bearings, at least that's the way I look at it.

JB: If I can just say briefly, one point on which I believe we agree—please correct me if I am wrong—is that we want to make strong normative claims that certain conditions are unlivable or that under certain conditions lives become unlivable, and under other conditions lives become livable and we want to be able to make that, but we don't want it all to be blurred, I understand that.

But I don't believe that livable and unlivable are a set of oppositions that exhaust the field, so if we go with the Derridian idea of living on, living on may or may not be livable. Living on was livable for a while, for Paul Celan for example, and then it wasn't. So, living on means that there is always a question of whether this is going to become livable or unlivable.

But I do think that it doesn't undermine the possibility of making a firm set of judgements to see that what you're calling a contradiction is actually lived in the course of a life, right?

Because a life can live contradictions, it can live in a contradictory way without solving the conceptual contradiction that structures that life. Usually when you live a contradiction, you live it as a tension, as an ambivalence, or perhaps through a certain kind of splitting.

FW: A polarity, right?

JB: Polarity is the friendly and hopeful way to say it. It's true.
I think, though, we need to distinguish between a contradiction at the conceptual level, which is nevertheless something
that can be experienced at the phenomenological level and
even endured at a phenomenological level, because it matters whether you are asking how a contradiction is lived or
whether a contradiction is valid. The second is a conceptual
question, the first refers us back to the phenomenological
moment and duration; more specifically, to the question of
what it is to live a contradiction in a life or to live a life that
is beset or besieged by contradiction.

Laure Barillas: I'd like to ask both of you a question that is
in the background of what you are talking about right now,
which is the answer to what the unlivable requires. You both
believe in the radical equality of human lives, but I wonder
if you don't perhaps envision different ways for achieving
this equality.

The impression I get from Frédéric Worms's reading is
that the care relationship might be an answer to the unlivable, whereas in Judith Butler's work, it takes the form of a
support network. One might therefore wonder whether this
difference between care and support, as two distinct ways of
responding to the unlivable, might not be in the backdrop of
your discussion.

JB: The issue of care is, of course, a large one in French
philosophical thought right now. It's with some trepidation
that I attempt to approach it. There are some aspects of the
argument about care that I certainly agree with. I think one
problem is that within the history of feminism in the United
States care was understood to be a maternal attribute and it

was elevated to a feminine and a feminist value which produced a certain idea of what mothers are or of what women should be—mothers should be caring; women should be mothers—which I thought was very conservative in terms of its gender politics. And it wasn't altogether livable for some of us, if I may use that word. (Laughter)

In some ways, the French discussion allowed me to reconsider the position (as does "The Care Manifesto" by Lynne Segal and Catherine Rottenberg, recently published in the U.K.). It took me a while to understand that in the work of Frédéric or Sandra Laugier or others, care has another valence and also in the more recent works of Joan Tronto—I see that her writing about interdependency and infrastructural support is very close to my own—so I think that's important. As long as care is not a gender disposition or a specifically feminine prerogative, as long as care is not simply a dyadic relation, modeled on mother and child, as long as care is relational, as I know it is for Frédéric, *and* also institutional, then I am able to understand it and work with it. What I worry about is that during a time when neoliberalism governs, in which social goods, social resources, social welfare are being decimated and outsourced, pensions are being destroyed or diminished, health care is becoming more difficult to acquire and afford in many places in the world (including the U.S.), when shelter is not guaranteed, food is being manufactured and distributed in a ways that are both toxic and unequal, I worry that we are sometimes asked to cultivate moral dispositions of philanthropy and "care" in a Christian spirit that will compensate for the institutional devastations that are wrought by neoliberalism. It should rather be the case that social services and provisions should be treated as public goods and public obligations that governments ought to honor. It doesn't always work that way, but it worries me that a certain kind of Christian value is elevated, one that tends to consolidate a very traditional notion of the family and women's care work, to compensate for these economic devastations and destitutions. Obviously, I don't want care to work in that way. I do not think it has to work that way. I think it could actually become closer to the principle of interdependency that I am trying to articulate. That's where I see the possible and potential convergence.

FW: Thank you. In the interest of brevity, I will start again from one of Judith Butler's essential books, *The Psychic Life of Power*,[2] and its paradox, which is in some ways the opposite of the paradox of *care* but is in fact complementary to it. There's the idea in Judith's work that the emergence of subjectivity depends on a power that "creates" us, so to speak, and that can also destroy us. For me, this is essential because it recognizes our original dependence on power. But this is what care means. Care is not necessarily benevolence: these are primary relationships that make us what we are, for better but also possibly for worse.

It can be for the better (or the worse) precisely because the care relationships we depend on are polarized, ambivalent, and also social, caught up in political frameworks where we can encounter the polarity of the livable and the unlivable. For this reason, care is not always benevolent in my view. It is traversed by the risk of violence or, rather, what I call *violation*. And the philosophical reception of care in France has also been collective and polarized: the two extremes are Levinas and the relationship with others, but also Foucault and medical power. Between the two, the thinker of polarity remains Canguilhem with his notions of the normal and the pathological, care and power. These polarities intersect with social relations, with discriminations: for example, care is often taken to be feminine and power masculine, as in the polarity between nurse and doctor. But the fact is that all relations of power, whether social or racial, are to be found within care, wrought by its inherent contradiction. This is why, in my opinion, and I don't think I am far off from Judith in this respect, care and power are able to respond to the threat of destroying subjectivity that they contain.

This is what allows us to rebuild subjectivity, without any guarantee of resilience and with the risk that this restoration may be impossible, which is precisely the threatening reality of the unlivable, of the impossibility of reliving, of the irreparable. But if there were no care and empowerment in vital relations, whether we call it care or otherwise, there would be no hope for justice, for recovery through institutions, for the effect of criticism as well, which is a struggle in care too. This is because even the most intimate care is traversed with violations and the risk of violation, even in parental relations. There are both paternal and maternal violations, of course!

Some dictators claim to be "bad parents." The bad father is proud to be authoritarian and violent; the stepmother also occupies a place of fascination in our collective unconscious. We see it in fairy tales, which is no coincidence. I certainly do not idealize care. On the contrary, I think that it should be viewed critically, and that is why I defend a critical vitalism but also a critical humanism. Ambivalence and polarity are everywhere, making criticism necessary everywhere. There is power everywhere, but it is polarized, even in humanitarianism, for example, and even in democracy, which is the most divided and explicitly critical regime in the world.

When it comes to those who fail to criticize care practices, you would be right, your criticism would be on the mark. But if we criticize them, we rediscover that which is vital: medicine, justice, and even love and friendship.

JB: May I ask one question? To what degree is your conception of care dependent on a psychological account of childrearing that depends on the framework of Winnicott?

FW: To the highest degree! *(Laughter)*

JB: OK. So, the childrearing scene becomes the model for thinking about broader social and political relations?

FW: Ah, I depend entirely on Winnicott, but on Winnicott's work as a whole, including his thought on the negative and on culture, politics, and democracy. He also wrote about adolescence, rebellion, violence, and aggression. We cannot reduce Winnicott to primary care and the mirror of the maternal face: his work must be taken as a whole. When Winnicott speaks about adolescence and aggression, and how only democracy makes room for them, it is because he recognizes the original role of conflict. He reflected on the generational revolt of the 1960s like no one else. He can't be reduced to his thought on primary love: he was a reader of Melanie Klein on hate and aggression. He's no Winnie the Pooh—his own play on words, by the way, since he invented the concept of the transitional object or security blanket!

JB: My concern is that for Winnicott paternal care could never be "good enough" in the way that maternal care can be. And I also think there are presumptions in that work about family structures, kinship, adoption, blended families, as well as a sanitized scene of childhood care. For children who have multiple parents or who go through several different stages of being cared for in different ways by different people, or if we think about this wonderful book in English called *All Our Kin*, which tracks African-American kinship

structures, which are very rarely dyadic and cross generations. Or when we think about contemporary queer and
trans kinship networks, which tend to have elements of
intimacy and solidarity as part of the scene. We see that the
shifting models of kinship actually make a difference in the
accounts that Winnicottians can give. Some of them are
trying to revise the position. And it's also important to know
he opposed mothers sending children to day-care. He was
critical of the so-called socialism of the day-care system in
the U.K.

FW: Understood. That's the risk of his historically dated
thought, but can we also point out the opposite risk, and the
person who ran it? Lacan, of course, with the name and law
of the father. It's true that love is not exclusively a matter of
the mother. Winnicott may have inadvertently prompted
this mistake. But the law is no more paternal than love is
maternal: each relationship must be regarded in view of its
critical polarity, between love and power.

JB: I agree. But I pose to myself this question, as well as to
you: Why start with the psychological scene of infantile
caregiving as the model for these broader questions of sociality, of economics and politics? Of course, the infant is
formed—you refer to the vital relations that form the infant.
But those parents who help to form the infant are also
formed socially and politically, and in language and society.
So where do we begin the story? There are a number of ways
of thinking about subject formation, and birth is one, but the
scene that led to the birth is another, as is the history that
precedes it. It matters, for instance, whether you were born
in a hospital and which one, whether you're born inside of
two people's marriage or outside a marriage, whether you've
got two or four or five parents . . . I mean, there are other

ways to start the story of the beginning of the subject's life. Who imagined you before you were born? Who never imagined you?

FW: You're quite right that a mythology of pure childhood should never serve as our foundation. "Everything" gets played out in childhood, it's true, but that doesn't mean that it's pure! On the contrary, it means that in childhood there's parental love and its polarity as well as the social structure, in which are entangled the mother, the father, history, the environment, the transmission of traumas, and everything else. We are born in a minefield, in a critical territory! And if you look at it from the perspective of the "end of life," the same would be true, as it would be for disease, or refugees . . . I certainly don't idealize vulnerability: it's actually a notion that I criticize. But the scenes of vulnerability are critical scenes that appear throughout the life course, which also show the limits of the livable. They are the most critical scenes, and it is from them that we need to start again.

JB: OK. Good enough. *Merci à vous!*

Paris, April 2018

Afterword (2022)

Frédéric Worms: Judith, this time, you went directly to contemporary issues, such as events.

Judith Butler: Yes.

FW: Events that are extreme and that make demands both on our moment and on our thoughts and our concepts. And I wondered, how do you think the livable and the unlivable are tested by events? You see what I mean? You ask what is livable about the refugee condition, and I think if there has to be a criterion for distinguishing between the livable and the unlivable, which there does for me, what kind of a criterion is it? How do we apply it to events?

JB: Yes.

FW: And situations? Maybe this is too much of a methodological question, but it's . . .

43

JB: No, it's an important question. I think one issue is: Do we start by setting up criteria and discuss those criteria at a theoretical level and ask what justifies drawing the line between the livable and the unlivable? And then do we apply the theory to empirical examples, or do we learn something about the unlivable and the livable from these events, from these ways that people undergo displacement or flight or bombardment or hunger? In other words, do we get a new sense of what is unlivable or is it the case that an historical view misunderstands that the livable and the unlivable are conditions that are relatively ahistorical? That is, should we proceed as if it's an operative distinction that holds true no matter what the circumstance? I mean, I'm just thinking that when Freud wrote his reflections on war in 1915, he was suggesting that something historically new had happened with the development of mass death and trench warfare, and that it had been unprecedented that so many lives were killed in war and by those means. And he, of course, had no idea what was coming. He was already overwhelmed by the experience of the First World War before the full destruction was known. So, did that make him think differently on life and death, on the limits of the livable?

FW: Yes, I think so. Of course, the considerations on war and death turn his work toward life and death in general and to the life and death drives. But then again, maybe he analyzed war through psychic impulses because he had this theory before. He's also been accused of depoliticizing the war, which he didn't actually. My point also is it's true that we learn something from the refugee situation or the Ukraine war or the new extreme historical experiences of unlivability. At the same time, I think it's a test for these categories, because I was thinking about your question about the refugees, and I think it is analyzable within the categories of the livable and the unlivable. But I think we have to clarify and reclarify these notions and work out how they are produced by different situations. What I mean is, if we treat questions of the livable and unlivable in biologically reductive ways, we will tend to reduce the refugees to their capacity for surviving.

Whereas what strikes me immediately with regard to refugees, even allowing for the historical variety of refugee situations we're talking about, is that their position is both, so to speak, physically and psychically unlivable, and that this is entirely political. They are expelled from somewhere. They are broken off from a human and political frame, as you would put it. And we . . . the "we" thinking about them are in an entirely political relation to them. Livable and unlivable situations are relational categories. So, we have to differentiate among situations. Even if we feel they remind us, of course, of something that precisely Freud would call the original distress, so to speak, a primary helplessness.

JB: Right.

FW: You see what I mean. I don't know how you want to proceed, but maybe we can go now to the situation. But I just wanted to make the point that it's not only from the situations that we learn about the categories, but it's back and forth.

JB: Yes. It is back and forth in the sense that new historical situations alter the categories by which we seek to grasp them.

FW: If we don't return at some point to what we mean by the livable and the unlivable, then we cannot understand what's happening rigorously.

JB: I think that's exactly right. But I'm just now thinking about Merleau-Ponty who has an argument about basic needs being the requirements of life. We could say that people need to eat, but food is organized in a certain way and eating always takes place in a specific way. So, there's always a modality that goes along with every basic need. People need shelter. They need to stay warm. We could say that's a biological need. And yet staying warm happens in many different ways. So even at the level of biological need, we find a certain social organization of need and of our life requirements. That means it's almost impossible to perform a biological reduction even if we were in a hospital and we remark that this person has lost body temperature, or this person is dehydrated. We are describing facts about the organism and trust that doctors are right to describe them as they do. At the same time, that person is thirsty in a certain context and in a certain way, and that person is losing body temperature under certain conditions and by virtue of a certain history. It may be as well that the medical framework differs according to which we describe what many of us call biology. So, the minute we start to describe how somebody came to experience something or what that experience is, we have the language they bring to describe the experience and the one that we bring, and a certain translation takes place. When we are referring to biological needs, we're also saying that needs are articulated in very specific social situations. When one reads Primo Levi's description of living in a concentration camp along with other people, and at one point, he tells us, somebody else wants the same piece of bread that he wants. They're both very hungry, and yet different kinds of relationships to the bread are possible. Some people will steal it no matter what. Some people will give it away easily or with difficulty. Some people will say "OK, you take this piece and I take this one." You know, the biological reduction to need is never fully complete or, when it is, it is also undergone in some very specific way.

FW: I don't know exactly. To me, it's even deeper in a way, because it's not only the opposition between, let's say, a biological need and an anthropological, cultural situation, which would not have anything to do with life, "their" lives, and "ours." Of course, there is no human need that is not culturally and anthropologically meaningful. But it's even deeper. For example, take today's refugees and victims of the wars. They're obviously deprived of something by other human beings. For example, in the Primo Levi situation, it's not only that he's hungry. He is deprived of food by some power; that hunger is produced.

JB: Yes. Yes. Induced precarity.

FW: I think what we need to understand is that what we represent to ourselves as unlivable in these kinds of situations—it's not only physical suffering or biological suffering. It's the conditions of the suffering which are humanly produced. And I think that the "we" who is *thinking* about them is important. You brought up Freud immediately, which is quite interesting because, to me, at the same time we identify with these people, refugees, for example, or with what the testimonies of the camps describe, we also have an impulse to differentiate ourselves from the situation.

This is why—and I don't know if it's natural—but there's ambivalence. And this is also, I think, why the refugee situation is contemporary with the extension of borders, of walls. Because there is this deadly impulse to protect ourselves from situations we know are unlivable for others. What is this kind of "thinking about someone"?

JB: Precisely.

FW: And so there is this vicious circle that we represent. We feel that this unlivability is produced, and instead of criticizing what produces it, there is something activated in some people and probably in everybody—a tendency to aggravate it.

JB: Yes, there is.

FW: So how do you explain that in the face of a situation where there are so many refugees, the reaction is, let's say, ambivalent. We, here, we want to resist this. But something also aggravates the situation. The more refugees there are, the more borders, the more rejections, and then the more refugees again. For me, livable and unlivable are not simple biological categories. They are intricate and ambivalent, and they go together with a set of emotions. You could, of course, understand these situations without these categories [of livable and unlivable] but not at the same levels, or in the same ways.

JB: Yes. But it seems like you're also saying that something about the unlivable makes us turn away or makes it worse.

FW: And this "us" and "me" have to be questioned, of course.

JB: Yes. We are both speaking from global situations of relative peace and security. So, let's just hold the "we" open for a moment. Something about the unlivable makes us turn away because we don't want to imagine that we could be in that situation. And yet we know we could. And that denial intensifies the suffering.

FW: Yes.

JB: In principle, it could happen. I mean, people in Ukraine did not think they were going to be bombarded or killed or brutally forced from their homes or see their loved ones die. I mean, that was not in their minds, even those who knew that a Russian military assault was possible. This is, I think, one reason why Ukraine is so unsettling for Europe. It's like, wait, that's us. This is us? This could happen to us?

FW: Yeah, exactly.

JB: But if I understand you correctly, you're also saying that the turning away reproduces the situation. It's almost impossible to turn toward it and to stay there, once having turned toward it. Right? Without looking away, without refusing it at some level. But this ambivalence is also part of its reproduction.

FW: I think so. I think it's complicated, but that's because I think it would be too simple to say, "we feel there is something unlivable here" and then analyze the situation and someone says, "OK, if it's unlivable for them, then we want to repair, help, care." Of course, it's ambivalent even in Rousseau—"*pitié*"—compassion? Or pity?

JB: Yes. In English, we argue about the translation. It's generally pity or compassion.

FW: It's a minimum.

JB: OK.

FW: Rousseau says that when a horse sees a dead horse on the road, it turns away. And he says that humans have a natural compassion, but we also have a natural tendency to turn away from compassion.

JB: Yes. Or we turn against our compassion. Or perhaps we think we're turning toward life, but maybe we're turning away. I don't know. It's interesting to think about it as something that both animals and humans do.

FW: Simone Weil also says that *"le malheur"*—misfortune or misery—produces a reaction of *"dégout,"* of hatred or disgust. We have a feeling of repulsion before the unlivability of others.

JB: Yes, we sometimes do. It is one part of the ambivalence you are describing.

FW: I think the extension of unlivability today confronts us with this ambivalence at an unexpected level. We want to solve the problem, the unlivability, even for nonhuman living beings, but the scale of unlivability also produces a reaction of overprotection, walls, borders, exclusion, separations . . . It makes matters worse because we're talking about unlivability that is humanly produced and are then producing more. And we know in a way that this is what we are doing. This is why, for me, being a living being is being ambivalent. Life and death are within us. They're not only outside.

JB: Yes. And I think it's interesting, as the pandemic eases—I don't believe it's over, but let's say it's easing in certain parts of the world—the desire to be done with it is a very strong desire. Even very smart people eagerly proclaim that the pandemic is over, that we don't need to worry about infection anymore. Their reasoning has three basic steps: We suffered. We're done suffering. We're now free to resume daily life. But as we resume daily life, there is the question of those who remain vulnerable, the immunocompromised, those who still cannot move as easily in the world because of their physical conditions, their susceptibilities. Are they to be abandoned or sacrificed in the name of the "many"? If so, we have become cruel utilitarians.

This discussion returns us to the question of climate change and the way we are living now. We continue to use this "we" even though there is no one plurality, but perhaps the "we" implicates us all in the fate of the earth. In the face of climate change, so many of us look away. I mean, we know it, we talk about it, and we lament it. We wish someone would do something about it, but we also look away in order to have some form of enjoyment that we want to have, that we feel is our right or our way of life, if we have one that has remained relatively untouched. Of course, for some people living in the middle of climate change, in Indigenous lands in Brazil, for instance, human interventions into their life worlds have produced toxic soil and the inability to drink the water that is available to them or grow the crops they require, the ones they have grown for generations. Their political resistance is, of course, political and very strong, both against corporate extractivism and against environmental destruction. Even then, I think, for those of us who are in more privileged positions, we might learn about that, we might see what's happening, we might understand what's happening to the air, to the soil, to the water, knowing full well that we rely on all those things as well, and use our positions to demand change. And yet many of us turn away from what is destroying the fundamental elements of life, including potentially our own lives and our own way of life. It's extremely hard to put that together in a way that is not utterly paralyzing. But that remains the task.

FW: You said very important things in there. What strikes me is that we go from an extreme to another. The "we," again, is very important. We want to be done with the pandemic. So, something in us wants to be done. And it's complicated, whether it's a life drive or a death drive thinking that way.

JB: Yes. The quick move toward life, the one based in denial, turns out to be further death.

FW: And yet, we want to be done. And, what you add very rightly, that's justice itself. You want to say that even if we are done, some people are not done—the more vulnerable, those who remain vulnerable. We turn away from climate change as a universal danger, we look away—I like this phrasing—but we know that some people are more vulnerable than others, and their worlds are already being destroyed. It is not just a future prospect. And in both cases, climate and with the pandemic, when we think we are done, or when we concede that some people are not done, what we refuse is the idea of a common vulnerability, a common vulnerability that *is* the pandemic and the climate and even the war in Ukraine, which serve as reminders that nowhere on earth are we protected from vulnerabilities.

JB: And that's unbearable in a way. I mean, we have fantasies . . .

FW: That's a new unbearability.

JB: Yes, I think that's right. The fantasy of overcoming vulnerability attests to the persistence of the condition; the fantasy blocks our confrontation with the unbearable yet attests to it.

FW: And at the same time, I think the only answer politically is to admit that these common vulnerabilities can build a new way of thinking of "we" and "them" and to acknowledge that the desire to be done with the pandemic is legitimate, vitally speaking. But we also have to admit that to be done with the pandemic should only mean fighting against the causes of the pandemic, the effects of the pandemic, fighting on the medical side, fighting on the social side, fighting for global public health. We have to change the desire to be done from a sort of passive drive for tranquility, which means, in the end, death. Instead, if the desire to be done with the pandemic is a desire to fight against negativities—failing healthcare but also environmental frailties and all the other social and economic failures that led to the pandemic—we will break with the idea that some are simply more vulnerable than others, and we are the protected ones. It's the same for the climate because we don't want to "look up"—of course, that movie, *Don't Look Up!* was interesting—no, we look away. That's because it's unbearable to think that the soil, the air, and the water are toxic.

JB: Yes. That the very conditions on which sentient beings depend in order to live have been destroyed by our uncaring interventions.

FW: In the refugee situation too, the ground is moving; as Foucault said, it's moving beneath us.

JB: Yes. We cannot know who is becoming a refugee as we speak, and how the numbers of the forcibly displaced will expand beyond the one-hundred million who currently are.

FW: Let us return to the concept of the toxic—it's a very interesting concept. I read some books on the environmental crisis and about toxicity, and I understand that something is toxic when it is structurally *"nuisible," "nocif"*—harmful, detrimental—when it produces an ill by virtue of its very essence. For example, you have a contingent situation such as air pollution. If you say the air is toxic, there is nothing to do. It is structurally killing you. What is killing you is in the air, has become part of what it is.

JB: This is an historically produced situation which becomes structural in time . . .

FW: It's just contingent pollution. So, a toxic environment is an environment that is structurally destroying you and not sustaining you.

JB: But then detoxification would involve structural change, right?

FW: Exactly. So, what do we do about that?

JB: Well. You know, I think we can go back to your remark that we seek to preserve ourselves, some "we," some group that calls itself "we." Whether or not we recognize that "we" is at issue for the immunocompromised who are missing the liberation from the pandemic. But there's also environmental destruction, environmental racism, which many people are already dealing with in their water, soil, and air. There's also the massive and expanding refugee population that is multiplying exponentially. Over a million people are refugees now in the world, according to UNHCR. You and I are not among the refugees. We are still, hopefully, breathing air that is decent and trusting the water that comes from our fountains.

FW: Right.

JB: Many people cannot. But for the "we" who seek to safe-guard ourselves, if I understand you right, this self-preservation is undertaken by a particular collective, but it's a particular collective that seeks to preserve itself *against* a general condition, or a condition that's happening else-where, and by separating itself from the generalized "we," it actually reproduces and intensifies the situation where a part of the world is abandoned, where toxicity can happen there, and a pandemic can happen there. It depends on intensifying inequalities for its "survival"—so is this a life drive or a death drive? This is the moment in which the ambivalence you describe is at work, this life-death impulse. In parts of Africa there have been very few vaccines. They're expensive. They're rare to find. Although we act as if we were not connected to those parts of the world. And "we" preserve ourselves by looking away from those places and building a literal or metaphorical wall around this collec-tive "we" that seeks to preserve itself. We cannot take dis-tance from the destruction without aiding and abetting in its reproduction, one that entails both heightened destruc-tion and loss, and intensifying social and economic inequal-ities. So maybe that is a necropolitical logic, one which allows toxification and destruction to go on elsewhere as long as it does not happen here. "There" and "here" become stabilized in the service of denial and abandonment. So if any of us subscribe to a version of the world in which such a radical inequality is affirmed and reproduced, or deflected from and reproduced, it follows that those who are preserving their way of life and assume their right to do so presume that there are others from whom they look away, but on whom they depend, or to whom they, or we, are invariably related, and who do not have that option to look away since destruction is, as it were, in their face. So, self-preservation, according to that logic, has a destructive set of implications, translating into "I will destroy to preserve myself. Even if I'm not going to war, I'm still destroying to preserve this collective which is partial, privileged, and protected."

FW: That's exactly the point. And I think what changed since our last conversation on the livable is precisely this generalization of unlivability.

JB: Yes. Can you say more?

FW: With the pandemic, with the intensification of the crisis of climate perception and reality, with the wars, this generalization is confirming the need for a philosophy of life and politics. What we see is that this generalization, this universalization, in a way, is one component of the critical vitalist position, that one reaches the universal through a generalized or common condition, by an empirical generality that's not only the abstract universal, but also a common planetary condition, so to speak. The concept of the planetary is quite interesting, too, because you don't approach critical politics only from the universal ideal as a point of departure, but rather from a concrete planetary condition. I think this generalized condition is also producing a sort of immunity reflex or denial. We spoke about denial the other day. I mean, pan-denial.

JB: Yes. The generalized condition does not directly lead to insight and a corresponding ethics, but also to new forms of flight and denial.

FW: Global denial. Because it's unbearable. It's unbearable to think, to start from the negative, the common negativities. To me, it's a very important question: How do we assume the common negativities when the pandemic concerns all of us? There is no we that will continue to be, there is no place that will be preserved against destruction. We didn't speak about economic globalization, the generalization of exploitation, which is inseparable from the, so to speak, effects of globalization on nature and conditions of health. So, if we think about all these global vulnerabilities, including the fact that we are vulnerable, even digitally, we are vulnerable to Twitter. The effect is so violent in a way.

JB: Yes. One reason to stay off social media as much as we require new networks for action. But are we making progress, and is progress still a goal, or part of the problem?

FW: We are used to a sense of progress, as we see in representations of history in Western philosophy, that says that we are not done, but we are going in some direction, and we will continue to help people who are more vulnerable. At the same time, we see growing injustice, and criticize its conditions. Now, we have to admit that we have to engage in a basic global struggle. To me, it's still a form of progress in a way, because the negative global conditions—the conditions of suffering and deprivation—remain our conditions. But how do we make something positive out of this very difficult awareness of global negativities, which indeed produce vicious circles? There is a major tendency toward separation, nationalism, sexism, and so forth, so the tendency to build a wall against these vulnerabilities is strong. The struggle is against the powers that produce these conditions, but also with that in ourselves which strengthen those powers, including our denial and our flight.

JB: I agree. We have to develop a collective practice of not looking away, or resisting conscious and unconscious collaboration with destruction. In a way, we've never needed . . . well, I don't know if this is true, but I'll say it anyway: we've never needed global governance more. International governance, health care, climate preservation, the rights of refugees.

FW: Economic regulation. Taxation.

JB: Yes. I mean, really, I do think that when we talk about common vulnerabilities, or what you call common negativities, they may be quite distinct from each other. At the same time, we cannot use those differences to deny commonalities, for we are also talking about a global interdependency that is nearly impossible to deny—or should be. This interdependency makes itself known (to those willing to know) under conditions of pandemic, climate change, and forcible displacement. We're interdependent. What happens in one part of the globe affects us here. We hear about a virus that starts in China. Next thing we know, it's in Italy. Next thing we know, it's in France, in New York. And I'm locked down in San Francisco.

FW: And even in Ardèche!

JB: Yes, in Ardèche. But when we talk about this interdependency, it's very strange because it's not the idea of intimate dependency in the sense that, oh, I depend on these people to be well, or I depend on these people for my food. There's not a person or a structure that I know intimately, and yet I am still intimately at risk. I feel my risk as an intimate reality. I will get ill, or I may not get ill, or I can't breathe in certain cities, and I can't go there. Or if I do go there, I need oxygen. China is actually doubly afflicted in this way given the pandemic and given the air quality. It's a health situation of enormous seriousness.

And yet, I do think that fathoming our interdependency without an idea of intimate dependency is very hard to do. Yet it's true about supply chains—some people are trying to build a home, and they're not able to build it because they cannot get basic supplies because production has slowed under the pandemic. Conditions of labor are intimately connected with conditions of health. I wonder whether we are, in effect, being asked by these global conditions to think how we might think about health care and climate politics outside the nation state, outside the national frame. Because, as you say, those borders do not protect in the way that they claim to. They actually reproduce the issue. They aggravate it through the production of social inequality on a global level. So, I wish that there could be a global movement for global health care. For that we must ask, What are the basic provisions? What does every human creature on this earth require? How might we go about making sure they all get it? Of course, there would immediately be great resistance, not just from nation states, but medical associations and corporate health care, regional blocs like the European Union, maybe, or the U.S. sphere of influence invested in certain markets. I mean, I could just imagine a state's response of "No, nobody will tell us what to do. We are a self-determining nation state." And yet, that's a form of self-determination that has to be limited by an understanding of our interdependent condition, understood globally. We're not just dependent upon one another in our practices: the way someone else practices in another part of the world affects me. Of course, the corporate and manufacturing centers of the world also have to own up to their specific responsibility for destroying the climate. But we're also dependent on animals and other life forms. And we are part of a broader ecological set of interrelationships, which moves us out of the anthropocentric point of view and even beyond the nation state as the ultimate form of political governance. So, I do wonder whether there will emerge, or is now emerging, some more global movement to establish governance on both health care and climate change. I don't think there's another way around it. There's global governance on refugees. I mean, we have international accords, even though signatories are breaking them all the time. The European Union is breaking them all the time.

FW: A global movement for global health care is very important to me, and I am very glad to hear you talk about it. What strikes people about this kind of phrasing is that it's too big—but I don't think that it is. Why would it be too big? And I want to bring in a concept—and I don't know if you will agree—but to me, it also goes back to gender questions and livabilities. It's the concept of the minimal. I wrote a paper for the online journal *AOC* during the pandemic that was called "The Minima of Vital Democracy."

JB: Yes, I received it.

FW: Right. And, for me, the concept of the global is linked to the concept of the minimal.

JB: OK. Say more.

FW: If we think of a global state, not only is it impossible, but it's frightening in a way. But if we think of the global minimal requirements for life that are enforced by some institutions globally, then I think we have livability because the livable seems to be a minimal concept in itself.

JB: Yes, it is, truly. It is astonishing that the minimal is so difficult to achieve on the global level.

FW: Yes, this minimal concept of the livable is very important to all our lives. For example, the way I read *Gender Trouble*, its idea is to build a minimally livable life for every kind of life.

JB: Yes. I hope that is true.

FW: And this is revolutionary. The same applies to the idea of a global movement for global health care. Of course, I totally agree. But then I have to say, global health care is not only global in the sense of its geographic extension: it has to be global intensively, in all dimensions of human life. And for any of us to be healthy, we need not only to have food and water and so forth, but we need to lead a sexual life, an intellectual life, a moral life, and a political life. And so, we need to be recognized minimally in all dimensions of our lives. In all our lives.

JB: Right. That is well-phrased.

FW: This is a very serious issue for me. For example, in France, and I know it's the same elsewhere, perhaps in the United States too, people fear that after the viral pandemic, there will be a psychic pandemic, a pandemic of depression, of psychic health, so to speak. In France, we have this discussion about the differences between mental health and psychic health, which might be of interest to you.

JB: Yes, totally interesting to me.

FW: And there is this question of public mental health and public psychic health.

JB: I see. I would like to know more.

FW: It's very important because when you speak about global health . . . actually, the definition of health in the World Health Organization is quite interesting: "a state of complete physical, mental and social well-being, and not merely the absence of disease or infirmity."

So, it's a very global definition. Which people tend to think is unrealistic, but it's not unrealistic. It's unrealistic in the sense that being happy isn't easily achieved. We know that to be happy there are minimal conditions in all dimensions. It is impossible to be happy with only one set of conditions fulfilled. Amartya Sen, for example, is not very far from that in terms of his capabilities approach. But anyway, what I want to say is that, in the approach that focuses on the livable, the global has to be connected with the minimal.

JB: Yes. Well, maybe. That makes sense to me. It's funny that when I write about the livable, some of my friends say to me, "Oh, that's not very ambitious, right? Why can't we have emancipation?"

FW: I get that all the time! And you too, of course!

JB: Yes. But, you know, I never said, "only the livable and nothing more." But it's the precondition of everything more, right? So, it is the place of what we might understand as a general obligation to one another. I mean, I just think we're not obligated to make sure everybody is happy. We hope

they become happy. But happiness is very difficult to guarantee. Its conditions can be amplified, but they don't have
the power to make it happen.

FW: Yes.

JB: But surely nobody becomes happy if they are not at
least in some condition of livability. As you know, there's
the concept called "glocalism," which is a little different
from what you're saying, but what it suggests is that the
global cannot be thought apart from how it works in certain local situations. Yes, there's a global need for health
care, some global need to fight climate change. There's a
global, we can say, obligation that we have yet to live up to
on refugees. And the number of refugees increases drasti-
cally by the week, apparently, especially since the outset of
the war against Ukraine. But I think that we have to ask
how a globally shared condition functions in local places,
and how that in turn changes what the global looks like.
So, when I talk about international governance, I'm not
talking about a global state. And I think it's important to
remember that governance and state formation can be
separate. To ask, then, what are the institutional forms of
international governance and what do we make of covenants and contracts that assume states as signatories is
important, but so too are transnational networks and institutions that elude state control, and that address these areas
of common concern. For example, when a state signs on to
the Dublin Accord or an international accord on refugees,
it is obligated, but we can see how quickly those signatures
become empty when refugees are pushed back at sea by
those very nations. At such moments, non-governmental
organizations and networks assume the global responsibil-
ities that states have vacated.

FW: Did you see the Rwanda agreement with the British government, about two days ago, to relocate U.K. asylum seekers there?

JB: Yes. Intensifying displacement.

FW: Incredible.

JB: But when states do sign on, they say, "Our sovereignty ends here" or "Here, here's my signature, this is my sovereign agreement to become unsovereign in this regard, to yield or limit my sovereignty in this regard" for the purpose of acting in concert with other states to secure basic rights, to address fundamental needs. There's one point where Hannah Arendt actually says, look, states have been defined too often by their foreign policy, for example, by the need to defend their borders. The need for the state emerges from a foreign policy concern or is imagined as coextensive with it. But she counters, what if the state were nothing other than a set of treaties and covenants and contracts? Then its primary concern would be cohabitation and living with other states, which was her concern about the nation state and why she thought that strict boundaries could only reproduce statelessness, that the idea of a state based on national identity could only produce statelessness. I wonder what difference it would make if we could focus on international governments as always requiring a local implementation and organization. I am not imagining here a top-down power structure that imposes the global on the local instance, but as a convocation that sets the norms, even sets enforcement conditions, understanding that implementation is always a question of local actors working in tandem with each other and international norms in ways that make sense for the region. In this sense, there is always a practice of translation between global and local, and both terms change in the course of the exchange. Because for international governance to work, there have to be ways to assuage the fear that a mega state is going to restrict freedoms or impose an unwanted way of life.

I've been reading recently in the field of humanitarian studies, which, as a field, is actually just ten years old. The list of books they read is, of course, much longer, but humanitarian studies is committed to the idea that serving certain communities is not a question of an international organization imposing its will on local cultures, but rather working collaboratively with local people who have agency on the scene, in the scene, and who are interpreting and implementing certain kinds of norms for their local worlds, engaged in distribution, and engaging local communities as equals. There are very explicit efforts to try to ameliorate the hierarchies that we associate with international covenants, and perhaps that is different from what you're saying about the minimum. But if we agreed that there is a minimal set of conditions for livability, then the question of how that gets implemented and organized is a political question which may or may not involve states, right? It may or may not involve NGOs. But that brings us back to basic questions, I think, of global governance in a way that's interesting to me. Through what established units does it work, and what kinds of new organizational structures does it require?

FW: Well, yes, I agree that, of course, you have to see international governance at a local level too. Before we address your question of how a globally shared condition functions in the local environment, I want to first go back to the question of agency. I think what we want to ask for is minimal agency for everybody. You have to remember, in my view, of course, that even the minimal is not guaranteed. We can be deprived of the minimal, and the minimal can be destroyed.

JB: Yes. I understand. How the minimal is cast or described seems crucial, and it may be less an isolated "need" than a complex sense of what life requires in a particular language or lifeworld. Yet, what is called the "minimal" is crucial for so many other political and social concepts and possibilities.

FW: I would argue that even agency has minimum conditions. This also brings us back to what you said about people telling you that the livable is not enough, which is true. But if it's minimal agency, then of course, in itself, we understand that this is the condition that allows us to go further, because you enable people to go further—by themselves, which is crucial. That's one point, because the agency question is very, very important, because when you speak of minima and the livable, you always think of an institution guaranteeing conditions of livability to others top-down, so to speak. But conditions of livability also require certain conditions for a subjective life, and this brings us back to the theme of this book, because I think what we defined earlier is the minimal subjectivity that makes life livable and death possible, even when the body is alive. We can face situations that are "worse than death" or that evince "death in life." So, that's another point. At some time we have to go back to death, so to speak. As for the state, I think what I would add to your description of the local implementations of the global—and I think it goes back to a lot of your work—that the borders of the state are not only external. They're internal.

JB: Yes. That is important to describe.

FW: If you want to preserve yourself from vulnerabilities, a tendency is to create a border, or a lot of borders within a population, separating one part from another. So, to me the globally shared conditions are local because the differences in vulnerabilities are inside a single country, a single city, even a single street maybe, where you have neighbors. I just realized that one of my neighbors had a very serious case of COVID and I didn't even know. She just fainted in her apartment nearby. You may have people with diabetes or a chronic disease in your street.

JB: In your street without knowing.

FW: And you don't know.

JB: Yes. Because an effective partition exists, whether material or otherwise.

FW: And you might realize that you did not take "care," really.

JB: Yes. You have not cared, because the conditions of care were not put in place. No one cared enough to put them in place.

FW: You know, there is this association for people on dialysis in France. It's a very strong association, called Renaloo. And the people they represent, people on dialysis, they're locked down. They are still locked down. For them there is no going out.

JB: No emancipation for them.

FW: So, the borders are also inside. And another example. I read an article in the paper this weekend written by a Black woman in France. And she wrote, "Thinking about not voting next week—not voting against Marine Le Pen—is a luxury for

White men. As a Black woman, I can't afford this, because I know it will worsen the situation in very, very concrete ways."

JB: Oh. Wow. "I can't afford this," yes, that's very interesting, asking who can afford not to vote.

FW: The situation is not good, but if you don't vote, it will make it worse. And if you are a White man, maybe your daily life will not change that much under Marine Le Pen. But if you are a Black youth, it's not easy to take the Métro, given the police presence. Today, if a policeman says, "I acted in legitimate defense," there is an inquiry. Le Pen just said she would lift these kinds of self-defense trials if she became president. She said she would consider *a priori* that policemen are acting in self-defense.

JB: Oh, my God.

FW: Whatever you do, the policemen shoot. As policemen, *per se*, they are supposed to be acting in self-defense. Which is not possible to say a priori, because it has to be checked and stated through trial and by a tribunal, under rule of law. So, I connect this declaration by Marine Le Pen to this Black woman's statement saying, "You intend not to vote next week? That's a White man's luxury."

JB: Yes, it's interesting.

FW: And I connect that with the local, the globally shared conditions from the inside: because we have the pandemic inside, we have climate change inside, we have inequalities about living close to chemical plants, for example. I have a house in Normandy that's not too far from a nuclear plant.

And as part of the local population, I was recently advised to get some iodine pills, to protect ourselves from radiation. So, this is local vulnerability . . .

JB: Yes, indeed!

FW: . . . if you live in France. There are nuclear plants all over the country.

JB: Yes. Throughout Europe.

FW: So that's how I understand globally shared conditions in the local environment.

JB: Yes. But it is interesting to look up from one's small life within a relatively privileged world and to see that the risk that is nearby or the problem with the soil next door or the person on dialysis, that all this is a repetition of what's happening elsewhere and often in more intensified versions. And to allow the local to become more general, to become part of a generalized condition about which we should all be deliberating, is also to try to ask how the general policies might be best implemented without the predictable forms of paternalism. It's hard to think of international governance structures without paternalism, but I think it must be done.

I want to ask you a question, and maybe this could lead us to a conclusion here. In the U.S. in the midst of the worst part of the pandemic, there were always those who said, "Well, I'm not going to wear a mask" or "I'm not going to obey any protocols of safety, because that is a matter of personal liberty, and it is my life."

FW: Yes, liberty was the watchword of the pandemic.

JB: Yes, yes. And "This is my life." Thus, separate from another's.

FW: "My life." And "Let me die if I wish."

JB: "Let me die if I wish." But usually, they didn't take into account that they might be letting someone else die, too, right? They could be spreading a lethal virus to those who are vulnerable, or somebody's grandmother might end up being affected. So, I think there has been a kind of death drive at work in the idea of personal liberty. But, you know, the death drive also usually acts in a fugitive way, attaching to something else that doesn't look like death—that might even go by the name of life.

FW: Exactly.

JB: So, here's the situation where this is my life. I could have a gun. I can kill whomever I want who trespasses on my property, even those I perceive or imagine to be trespassing. My property is my personhood, and my self-defense extends to my property. Similarly, one lays claim to one's life to say, this is my life, I will not wear a mask for reasons of public health. And, as a further extension of my personal liberty, I am free to infect everyone and too bad if people die. Too bad if I die. This is my life. At least, I die free. All this is how the death drive in personal liberty sounds to me under these conditions.

So, I guess, this is a question for you. Could we make a distinction between critical and uncritical vitalism on the basis of different ways of acting in accord with a sense of life, acting in accord with even a principle of life? Because those who say, "This is my life, I will do what I want, even if it kills others or risks my own life," are probably in the grips of the death drive, doing damage in the name of life. In some ways, that seems like life to them. Right? But then life as related to common vulnerability, to interdependence, to establishing the minimum of what is required for livability—this is all part of what you call critical vitalism. It's perhaps knowing about the false ways that a claim of life can appear. To counter such a claim, one should insist, in my view, that life itself has to be understood less in terms of a version of personal liberty that comes at the expense of others, and more fully in terms of what I would call interdependency, or what you might call an ethics of care. I don't know. But it would be good to hear you on that topic.

FW: Well, thanks, because it brings us back to the central concern of this conversation, and it's very important not to avoid that issue at the end of this part of our ongoing conversation. Of course, I don't know what life is. The first gesture of critical vitalism is to criticize any independent concept of life. I know life only as it is opposed to death. And the gesture of critical vitalism is critical in at least two senses: life is always to be understood in opposition to something else (it must be critically distinguished from what it opposes) and any tendency to go beyond this opposition must also be critically questioned. As in any critical philosophy, beyond a certain limit lies delirium, so to speak. And to go beyond a sort of opposition between life and death— life as opposed to its interruption, as opposed to its negation, its negative pole—means to go, as Kant would put it in his *Critique*, toward its transcendental dialectic or illusion. So, the moment you think of life without the opposition to death, you're in an illusory domain. A critical concept of life would never lead you to say, "Too bad if I die," in the sense of "Who cares?"—in the sense that is associated with the death drive.

JB: Right. I agree.

FW: And the death drive is precisely another dimension of critical living, in that we live against death as an internal enemy—that is, not only as an external risk, but as an internal adversary. And so, we never stop wrestling with this internal criterion of living against something that drives us, even in the name of life toward death. And, of course, we know that religions of love can be hateful if they speak of love without an internal fight against hate. You know, just as there is no pure love without hatred, so there is no life without the internal drive to death?

JB: Yes, but sometimes the internal drive to death calls itself life.

FW: True. And the internal drive for hatred calls itself love. You hate in the name of love because you hate in the name of love without a contrary. Because love without a contrary brings us to hatred, in a way.

JB: Yes. I see what you are saying. It will be counter-intuitive for some.

FW: And the moment you forget about the contraries you fall into an abstract unity, which is destructive. And so, of course, you never say "Too bad" if people die—"Too bad" in the sense of "Who cares?" Because it's just plain bad if people die, not bad in the sense of "too bad." It's an interesting expression because you say something is bad but in actuality you neutralize it. No, I think, really, we have the distinction between life and death as an ultimate criterion. I just wrote a paper about that in *Libération* last week, for the election, and I compared it with the ultimate end-of-life choices: euthanasia, and so forth, and the "worse than death" concept from Adorno to Derrida and Lyotard. For me, when Derrida and Lyotard say that there are "worse than death" situations, that comparison can make death into a relative good as opposed to "worse than death."

It doesn't weaken death as the criterion for distinguishing between what is ill and what is good. It just says that there are situations that can be worse than death, meaning that death remains the criterion even for something worse than death itself. You see what I mean? And so, the death question. The moment you allow a death to happen that you could have avoided, whether yours or someone else's, you contradict the meaning of life in general. I think that it's a general, let's say, betrayal . . . But it's a general violation that is also a defeat, so to speak. So how do we reintroduce what you call grief or grievability? We reintroduce it as a criterion for life—a life should be established as grievable—when you come to admit that a death remains unmarked or not considered a death at all, that its loss does not produce grief for that life. And it doesn't . . . To me, when you study grievability, it's a literal concept. It's not a metaphor.

JB: Yes. Can you say more?

FW: This is a critical vitalist approach because it does put life in the context of ethical and political relationships, which is its natural place.

JB: Which is its natural place, meaning the place where it belongs.

FW: And loss and grief . . . Grief is typically a critical vitalist experience because if you are grieving, you're not dead, someone else is dead.

JB: Right. Grief is the prerogative of the living.

FW: And the death of one person has an effect on the life of another. But, of course, grief is the reverse of birth, the welcome given to new lives. Birth is also a situation where a life has an effect of another life. But it can and should be opposite to grieving, it can and must be a kind of welcoming. So, I think you're right to bring the death drive back into the discussion. I haven't addressed personal liberty yet, but it's the same, of course. In the name of liberty, you can destroy everything else, whereas liberty is really felt when it is threatened. There is a risk about it, because the idea of liberty you talked about treats my life and life in general as the property of someone, whereas life is . . . I don't know what it is. I know what it is to care about the living. But I don't know how I can own my life. My own life.

JB: Yes. Yes.

FW: "This is my life." As if life were a good that you could use and dispense with—an objective good. Where is it, then? Show me your life!

JB: Ha! yes, yes.

FW: I want to do something with my life. Okay. Where is it? Decorate it, build it. No, you can't! Life is stories . . . When you say, "This is my life," to me it's more like a critical retrospection on a story. "This is my life with its blunders, with its mistakes, with its frailties, with its crimes, with its joys."

And you don't say "This is my life. I can do whatever I want with it" but rather, "This is my life. I have to assume responsibility for it." I don't possess it, but I'm responsible for it.

JB: Yes, that moves us beyond possession and property. But you would have to liberate life, in a way, from these categories—and maybe this is what your work is doing, Frédéric—you would have to emancipate life from personal property and individual liberty based on the idea of one's life as one's property and the idea that one gets to use it however one wishes. And maybe what you're asking us to move toward—and I agree with you here—is a more relational understanding of my life, your life, our life, the lives of others, with the mindfulness that life can never be lived or lived well without understanding the possibilities of destruction and death as right before us, as a struggle that defines the living. We cannot set death and destruction aside as we think about life, whether mine, or ours, or anyone else's. Or we cannot develop an idea of life that is predicated on a psychological denial of death. We need to oppose the forces of death in order to establish the conditions of livability, not just for myself, but for all.

FW: Right. It's like criticizing some uses of the concepts of life without renouncing what keeps a life from being lived . . .

JB: Right.

FW: I cannot do without living.

JB: No, no, you can't. You shouldn't.

FW: Who could?

Paris, April 2022

Notes

Preface

1. Judith Butler, *The Force of Non-Violence: An Ethico-Political Bind* (London: Verso, 2020), p. 196.

2. Frédéric Worms, *Pour un humanisme vital. Lettres sur la vie, la mort et le moment présent* (Paris: Odile Jacob, 2019), Lettre 43, p. 271.

3. This conversation took place at ENS—PSL under the auspices of the International Center for the Study of Contemporary French Philosophy (CIEPFC), a member of the République des savoirs Research and Service Group 3608.

4. A recording is available on the "Savoirs ENS" website under the title "Penser avec Judith Butler [Thinking with Judith Butler]."

5. The meeting, titled "Living today: the need for a critical vitalism," was organized by the Program in Critical Theory at UC-Berkeley.

6. We are extremely grateful to Claire Marin, whose contribution made this book possible.

Introduction

1. This conversation was preceded by a radio interview recorded the same day for the program "Matière à penser," broadcast on France Culture on May 14, 2018.

2. See "Qu'est-ce qui est vital," which appeared in the *Bulletin de la Société Française de Philosophie* in 2007, and "Pour un vitalisme critique," *Esprit*, vol. January, no. 1, 2015, pp. 15–29.

3. See *Gender Trouble: Feminism and the Subversion of Identity* (New York: Routledge, 1990) and *Undoing Gender* (New York: Routledge, 2004).

4. See especially *Frames of War: When Is Life Grievable?* (London and New York: Verso, 2016), and *Notes Toward a Performative Theory of Assembly* (Cambridge, MA: Harvard University Press, 2018). The most recent formulation of their social ontology of the living can be found in the postscript to their latest book published in English, *The Force of Non-violence: An Ethico-Political Bind*.

5. In *Rassemblement*, and *The Force of Non-Violence* and in *Les Maladies chroniques de la démocratie* (Paris: Desclée de Brouwer, 2017), and *Pour un humanisme vital* (Paris: Odile Jacob, 2019).

6. In *Rassemblement*, and *The Force of Non-Violence* and in *Les Maladies chroniques de la démocratie* (Paris: Desclée de Brouwer, 2017), and *Pour un humanisme vital*.

7. Georges Canguilhem, *The Normal and the Pathological* (Brooklyn, NY: Zone Books, 1991 [1943]).

8. "La vie dans la philosophie du XXe siècle en France," *Philosophie*, vol. 109, no. 2, 2011, pp. 74–91.

9. For more on this subject see the article by Frédéric Worms, "À quel soin se confier?" in Claire Marin (ed.), *À quel soin se fier? Conversations avec Winnicott* (Paris: Puf, 2015), pp. 37–48.

10. F. Worms, *Soin et politique* (Paris: Puf, 2012), p. 5.

11. Ibid., p. 43.

12. See *Gender Trouble* and *Undoing Gender*.

13. See *Precarious Life: The Powers of Mourning and Violence* (London: Verso, 2004) and *Frames of War: When is Life Grievable?* (London: Verso, 2010).

14. Here, the notion of life expectancy must be understood not only in its usual demographic sense, namely, the average life span, but also in a psychological and existential sense. Life expectancy thus refers to the capacity of the living to project themselves with confidence into the future, or to what Butler calls "an enduring sense of individual life, how life is endured, and with what degree of suffering, livability, or hope" (*Notes Toward a Performative Theory of Assembly*, p. 20). For convergent analyses of how life expectancy reflects the unequal social value placed on human lives, see Didier Fassin, *Life: A Critical User's Manual* (Cambridge, U.K.: Polity, 2018).

15. J. Butler, *Assembly*, p. 117.

16. Ibid., p. 17.

17. J. Butler, *Frames of War* (London: Verso, 2009), p. 3.

18. J. Butler, *Assembly*, p. 110.

19. Ibid., pp. 21–22.

20. F. Worms, *Soin et politique*, p. 16.

21. J. Butler, *Frames of War*, pp. 21–22.

22. F. Worms, *Les Maladies chroniques de la démocratie*, Introduction.

23. F. Worms, *Revivre* (Paris: Flammarion, 2012), p. 309.

24. F. Worms, *Les maladies chroniques de la démocratie*.

25. On this reinterpretation of the liberty, equality, fraternity triad in the light of "critical vitalism," see F. Worms, *Soin et politique*, pp. 35–36.

26. J. Butler, *The Force of Non-Violence*, pp. 94 and 100. On the relationship between a critique of hegemonic norms and their normalizing effects, and the defense of normative commitments, including the right to self-determination (interpreted as a condition of a livable life), see the first chapter of *Notes Toward a Performative Theory of Assembly*, "Gender Politics and the Right to Appear," pp. 24–65.

27. J. Butler, *The Force of Non-Violence*, pp. 100–101.

28. F. Worms, *Soin et politique*, p. 44.

The Livable and the Unlivable

1. Simone Weil, *Awaiting God*, introduction by Sylvie Weil, trans. Bradley Jersak (Abbotsford, BC, Canada: Fresh Wind Press, 2013 [1951]).

2. J. Butler, *The Psychic Life of Power: Theories in Subjection* (Stanford, CA: Stanford University Press, 1997).

Judith Butler is Distinguished Professor in the Graduate School at the University of California, Berkeley. Their books include *What World Is This? A Pandemic Phenomenology*; *The Force of Nonviolence*; *Toward a Performative Theory of Assembly*; *Precarious Life: The Power of Mourning and Violence*; and *Senses of the Subject*.

Frédéric Worms is Professor of contemporary philosophy at the École Normale Supérieure, Paris, where he currently serves as Director. He is the author of several works on critical vitalism and the ethics of care in French, including *La Philosophie du Soin* and *Soin et Politique*.

Arto Charpentier is a doctoral student in philosophy at the École Normale Supérieure (Paris). His dissertation explores debates regarding naturalism and social criticism in contemporary social philosophy.

Laure Barillas is Assistant Professor of Philosophy and French at the University of New Hampshire. She is a specialist in the work of Vladimir Jankélévitch, and her research focuses on contemporary ethico-political issues, with an emphasis on care and feminism.

Zakiya Hanafi is the author of *The Monster in the Machine: Magic, Medicine, and the Marvelous in the Time of the Scientific Revolution* and translator of books, among others, by Roberto Esposito, Simona Forti, Guido Mazzoni, Lorenzo Benadusi, Barbara Carnevali, and Francesco Zucconi.